Animal Camouflage

Hiding in a Coral Reef

Patricia Whitehouse

Heinemann Library
Chicago, Illinois

Designed by Cherylyn Bredemann
Printed and bound in the United States by Lake Book Manufacturing, Inc.
Photo research by Kathryn Creech

07 06 05 04
10 9 8 7 6 5 4 3 2

Library of Congress Cataloging-in-Publication Data
Whitehouse, Patricia, 1958–
  Hiding in a coral reef / Patricia Whitehouse.
    p. cm. -- (Animal camouflage)
  Summary: Offers a description of how animals living in a coral reef use various types of camouflage to survive, capture prey, or hide from predators.
    Includes bibliographical references (p.   ) and index.
    ISBN 1-40340-795-9 (HC), 1-40343-185-X (Pbk)
    1. Coral reef animals--Juvenile literature. 2. Camouflage (Biology)--Juvenile literature.
    [1. Coral reef animals. 2. Camouflage (Biology) 3. Animal defenses.] I. Title. II. Series:
  Whitehouse, Patricia, 1958–   . Animal camouflage.
  QL125.W45 2003
  591.47'2--dc21
                                        2002010279

Acknowledgments
The author and publishers are grateful to the following for permission to reproduce copyright material: p. 4 Georgette Douwma/Taxi/Getty Images; pp. 5, 10, 24, 28 Fred McConnaughey/Photo Researchers, Inc.; pp. 6, 7 David Behrens; p. 8 Amos Nachoum/Corbis; p. 9 David Hall/Photo Researchers, Inc.; pp. 11, 12, 13, 30T Robert Yin/Corbis; p. 14 Soames Summerhays/Photo Researchers, Inc.; pp. 15, 18 Stephen Fink/Corbis; p. 16 Christopher J. Crowley/Visuals Unlimited; p. 17 David Wrobel/Visuals Unlimited; p. 19 A. Whitte & C. Mahaney/Stone/Getty Images; pp. 20, 21, 30B Tom cHugh/Steinhart Aquarium/Photo Researchers, Inc.; p. 22 Mike Schick/Oxford Scientific Films; p. 23 Karen Gowlett-Holmes/Oxford Scientific Films; pp. 25, 27 Hal Beral/Corbis; p. 26 Fred Bavendam/Minden Pictures; p. 29 Jeff Rotman/Photo Researchers, Inc.

Cover photography by Fred McConnaughey/Photo Researchers, Inc.

Every effort has been made to contact copyright holders of any material reproduced in this book. Any omissions will be rectified in subsequent printings if notice is given to the publisher.

Some words are shown in bold, **like this.** You can find out what they mean by looking in the glossary.

To learn more about the pygmy seahorse on the cover, turn to page 5.

Contents

Hiding in a Coral Reef

Many animals live in and around coral reefs. Some coral reef animals are hard to see. They use **camouflage** to help them hide.

Some animals hide so they do not get eaten. Others hide from animals they want to catch and eat. There are many ways to hide. This pygmy seahorse has **cryptic coloration.**

Hiding on the Coral

A sea slug is hiding on this sponge. The slug is the same color as the sponge. Animals that look like their **habitat** have **cryptic coloration.**

Now the sea slug is on a sponge with a different color. It is easy to see. Other reef animals can find it and eat it.

Hiding in the Sand

Some coral reef animals hide in the sand. The blue-spotted stingray covers itself with sand to hide from **predators.**

Without the sand on top of it, you can see the stingray's spots. The stingray needs the sand to hide from other animals.

Hiding in the Water

Some coral reef animals look like the ocean water. **Anemone** shrimp have **transparent** bodies. They are clear just like the water. This makes them hard to see.

Many coral reef fish are transparent when they **hatch.** This is a young goby. Its small size and clear body help it hide.

Hiding by Looking Different

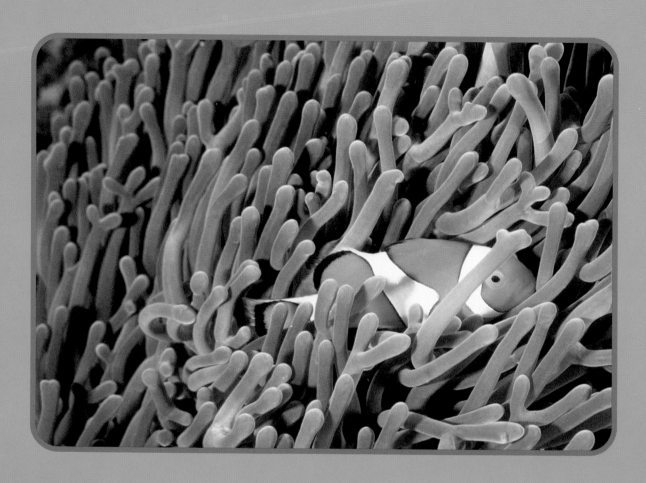

Some animals have color **patterns** that break up their shape. This is called **disruptive coloration**. The clown **anemone** fish uses its stripes to hide among anemones.

This **camouflage** grouper's body has dark and light colors. They hide the grouper when it is near coral. The colors make it hard to see the whole fish.

Hiding to Hunt

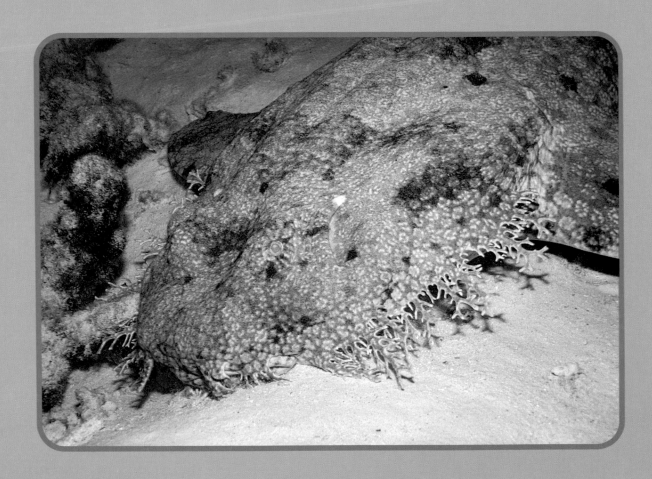

This wobbegong, or carpet shark, uses
camouflage to hunt. If it stays still, other
fish think it is the sea floor. They do not
see the wobbegong until it is too late.

The crocodile fish also hunts by staying still.
It hides in the sandy parts of a coral reef.
When another fish swims by, the crocodile
fish catches it.

Dark Above and Light Below

Some animals have dark backs and light bellies.
This is called **countershading.** Barracudas are
hard to see from above. Their gray backs look
like the dark rocks and coral below.

It is hard to see barracudas from below, too. Fish below a barracuda see its belly. The barracuda's light belly looks like the sunlit water above.

Hiding by Swimming

The sea turtle also has **countershading.** It can swim and hide at the same time. Its dark top shell, called the **carapace,** looks like the dark water below.

Predators below a sea turtle see its bottom shell. This shell is called the **plastron.** It is the same color as the sunlit water above.

Pretending to Be Another Animal

This is a banded sea snake. Its colors tell other animals that it is **venomous**. **Predators** stay away from sea snakes.

This banded snake eel is not vemomous. But it uses **mimicry**. It has the same shape and colors as a sea snake. Predators leave snake eels alone, too.

Hiding in Plain Sight

Some reef animals do not hide. They **mimic** things that **predators** do not eat. This reef octopus uses **cryptic coloration**. It looks like part of the coral.

These majid crabs are resting on a coral reef.
Their bodies have bright colors, and they are
shaped like coral. Predators might think they
are just another piece of coral.

Pretending to Be a Plant

This is not a piece of seaweed. It is a fish called the seaweed ghost pipefish. It looks and moves like seaweed floating in the water.

This leaf fish floats around coral reefs. Its colors and fins make it look like a dead leaf. This **mimicry** might trick a **predator**.

Changing Colors

Cuttlefish can hide in different places around coral reefs. They can change colors and **patterns**. This cuttlefish looks like the coral around it.

Now the cuttlefish is swimming above the sea floor. It has changed the colors on its body to look like the sea floor. The cuttlefish can change colors very fast.

Surprise!

A puffer fish has **disruptive coloration** that helps it hide from **predators.** But the puffer fish has another way to **protect** itself.

The puffer fish will surprise a predator by puffing up. Now the puffer is so big that it cannot fit in a predator's mouth!

Who Is Hiding Here?

What animals are hiding here?
What kind of **camouflage** do they have?

For the answer, turn to page 12.

For the answer, turn to page 21.

30

Glossary

anemone   animal that lives on a coral reef

camouflage   use of color, shape, or pattern to hide

carapace   turtle's top shell

countershading   top part of the animal is dark and the bottom part is light

cryptic coloration   colors that make an animal look like the place where it lives

disruptive coloration   pattern of colors on an animal that makes it hard to see the whole animal

habitat   place where an animal or plant lives

hatch   come out of an egg

mimic, mimicry   one animal looks and acts like a plant or another kind of animal

pattern   colors arranged in shapes

plastron   turtle's bottom shell

predator   animal that eats other animals

protect   keep safe

transparent   can see through

venomous   animal that puts a dangerous liquid into another animal

More Books to Read

Arnosky, Jim. *I See Animals Hiding.* New York: Scholastic, Incorporated, 2000.

Galko, Francine. *Coral Reef Animals.* Chicago: Heinemann Library, 2002.

Kalman, Bobbie. *What Are Camouflage and Mimicry?* New York: Crabtree Publishing Company, 2001.

Index